FELT TIP FUN

Acknowledgement

The authors, Carolyn Davis and Charlene Brown, would like to thank
all of the following for their patience and support —
Sally Marshall Corngold, Jim Paine, Kassie and John Raley,
and, of course, Sydney Sprague, editor,
and the rest of the wonderful staff at Walter Foster Publishing, Inc.

Introduction

Welcome to the fun world of felt tip pens! While most of us have used felt tip pens before, few of us have used them as an art medium. This is your chance to learn how to use felt tip pens for a variety of creative projects. The best feature of felt tip pens is that while they are easy to use, your art projects can look sophisticated and professional. You can even create a watercolor effect.

You will learn how to use felt tip pens on a variety of surfaces such as tin foil, plastic, various art papers, tissue, and more. Of course, the most important lesson we can teach you is that art is fun! Experiment with different types and colors of pens. Try the pens on different kinds of paper. Every time you do you will not only learn something new, but your art skills, as well as your visual and tactile skills will improve.

Note — the directions in this book tell what types of pens and papers (or other surfaces) we chose to use for our examples, but you can use any pens and paper you want — they're your projects!

Remember, **have fun** and use your imagination!

Glossary

ABSTRACT — A style of artwork with little or no attempt at pictorial representation. This means that instead of drawing an actual thing, such as a dog or a house, an artist tries to paint his or her emotions or state of mind. In this book, abstract art is used to help you become comfortable with felt tip pens as a medium.

BLEED — When colors spread out and/or run together, creating various effects, shades or even other colors.

HORIZONTAL LINES — Lines parallel to what would be the horizon; from left to right, rather than top to bottom.

MEDIA — Various materials used to create art. Paints, felt tip pens, pencils, etc. are all types of art media.

PERMANENT — Something that will last forever. In this book we use some felt tip pens that have permanent, or un-washable inks (see materials page).

SERIF — The small lines or strokes at the tops or bottoms of certain letter styles. Serif letter example: A. Sans serif letter example: A.

TEXTURE — The way something looks or feels. An object can have a smooth or rough texture, etc. In art, texture can make an object look more realistic or interesting.

THREE-DIMENSIONAL — Having the dimension of depth as well as width and height. A shoe box is three-dimensional.

TWO-DIMENSIONAL — Having only the dimensions of height and width (a flat surface). A picture drawn on a piece of paper is two-dimensional.

Contents

Materials

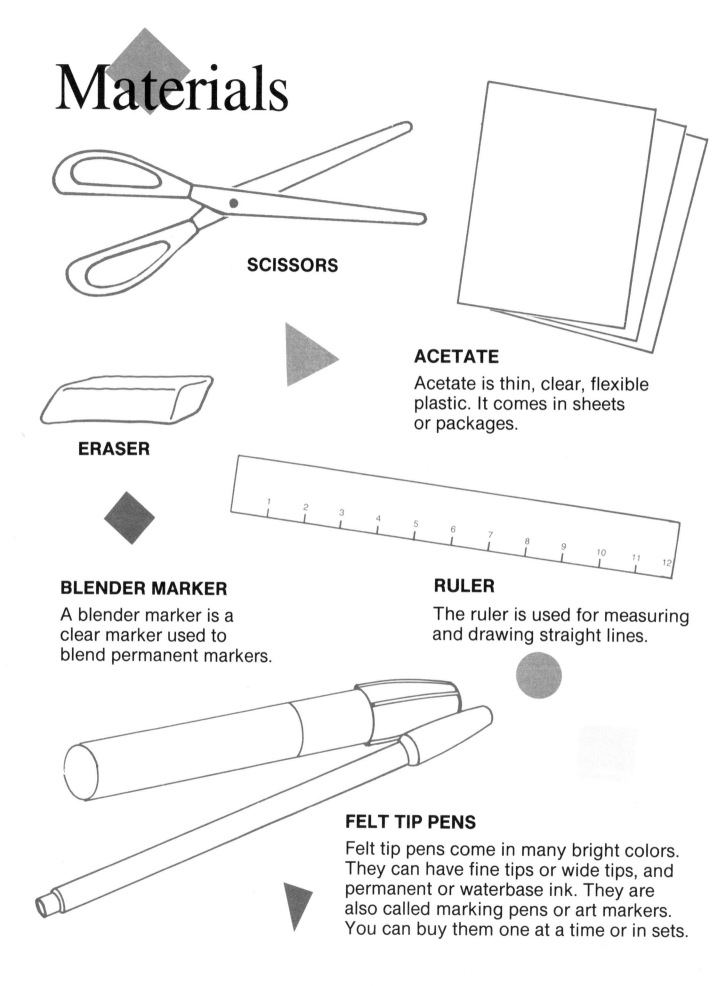

SCISSORS

ACETATE

Acetate is thin, clear, flexible plastic. It comes in sheets or packages.

ERASER

BLENDER MARKER

A blender marker is a clear marker used to blend permanent markers.

RULER

The ruler is used for measuring and drawing straight lines.

FELT TIP PENS

Felt tip pens come in many bright colors. They can have fine tips or wide tips, and permanent or waterbase ink. They are also called marking pens or art markers. You can buy them one at a time or in sets.

Materials, continued

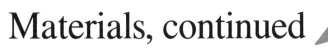

PAINT BRUSHES

There are many sizes and types of paint brushes. The best kind for the techniques used in this book is a medium sized soft-haired brush.

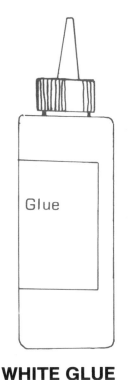

WHITE GLUE

PENCILS

TRACING PAPER

DRAWING PAPER

STRUCTION PAPER

PAPER

You will need watercolor paper, heavy white drawing paper and various colors of construction paper. Some of the projects call for newsprint, tracing paper, tissue paper, and smooth bristol board. These papers can be found at most stores that have school or art supplies.

1
COLORS AND TEXTURES

There are many types of felt tip pens and markers. They can have wide, thin, or fine tips, with either water-base (washable) or permanent ink. They come in every color of the rainbow and then some.

In this chapter we encourage you to experiment with many types of pens and papers. You may find you like one particular type of pen with one particular type of paper best of all. You may like using water-base pens best because you can create an effect that looks like watercolor paint. You may choose to make a variety of rainbows like we have. By using rainbows like we have used color wheels in our other books, you can see how the colors blend together and how they look next to each other. As you probably know by now, color may be the most important factor in art — so choose your colors carefully!

Experimenting like we have done in this chapter is the best way to learn about texture and color. Remember, **have fun** and use your imagination! You'll never know what you can create until you try!

Rainbow Of Colors

Wide Markers

The best way to learn how different markers look on different papers is to experiment — have fun making rainbows!

We used wide markers to create these solid colors. You may choose permanent or water-base markers. When filling in a solid area, make even, straight rows with the widest part of the marker, as shown.

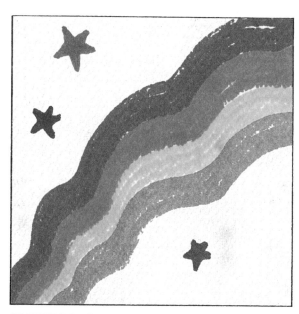

WATERCOLOR PAPER

SMOOTH BRISTOL BOARD

HEAVY DRAWING PAPER

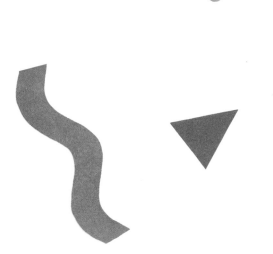

10

Thin Markers

Here we used thin markers to create a lighter effect. You may choose permanent or water-base markers.

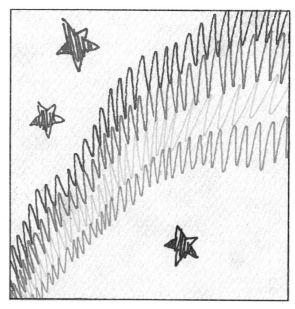

WATERCOLOR PAPER

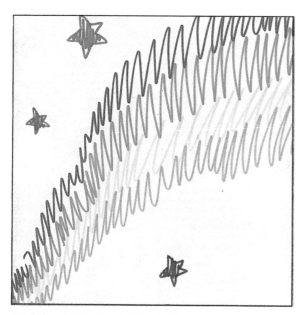

SMOOTH BRISTOL BOARD

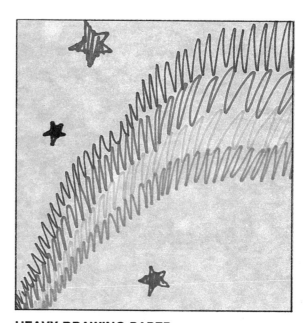

HEAVY DRAWING PAPER

11

Wide Water-Base Markers

Here we used a paint brush and water to paint over wide water-base markers to create a soft watercolor effect. The water causes the ink to bleed, as shown.

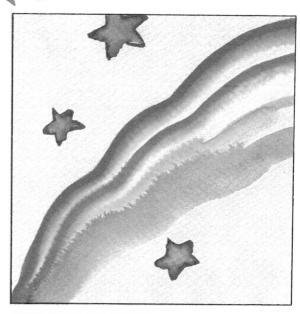

WATERCOLOR PAPER

SMOOTH BRISTOL BOARD

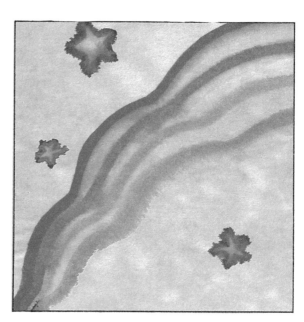

HEAVY DRAWING PAPER

Thin Water-Base Markers

Use a paint brush and water to paint over thin water-base markers to create a different watercolor effect.

WATERCOLOR PAPER

SMOOTH BRISTOL BOARD

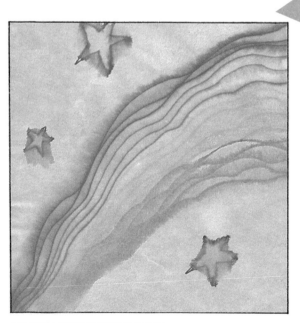

HEAVY DRAWING PAPER

Blender Markers

Use a blender marker (see materials page) and permanent markers to soften and blend colors together.

TRACING PAPER

SMOOTH BRISTOL BOARD

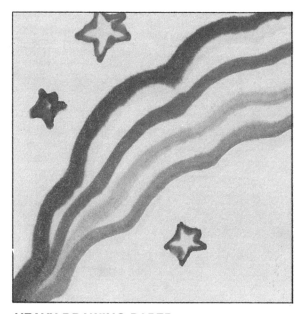

HEAVY DRAWING PAPER

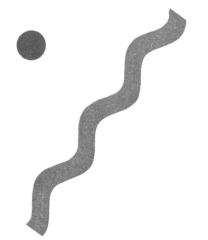

Wide and Thin Markers

Use wide and thin markers together to create a variety of designs.

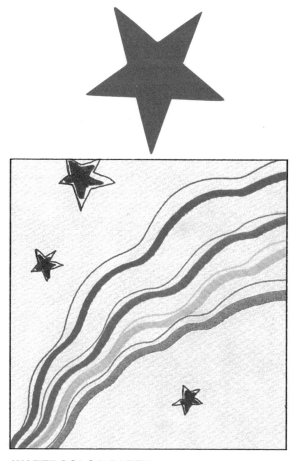

WATERCOLOR PAPER

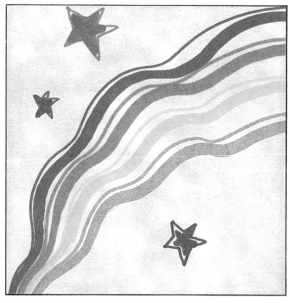

SMOOTH BRISTOL BOARD

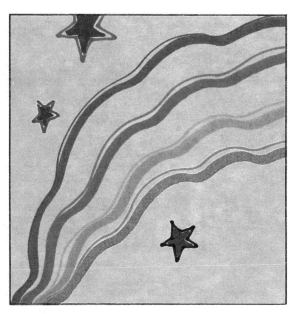

HEAVY DRAWING PAPER

Abstract Rainbow

Draw the same design with different felt tip pens
to create a variety of effects.

1 Use light pencil to draw your
design on a piece of watercol-
or paper.

2 Trace over the pencil lines
with a thin permanent marker.

3 Use permanent markers to
color the areas of your design
that you want to remain solid.

4 Use water-base markers to
color the areas of your design
that you want to bleed (see
glossary on page 4).

5 Use a wet paint brush to paint over the water-base marker areas. The water-base colors will bleed and blend together while the permanent marker colors stay solid.

6 You may choose to frame your picture by gluing or taping it to a piece of colorful construction paper.

2
LETTERING

One of the most common uses of felt tip pens is lettering. You usually see felt tip pens used for plain, block printing which isn't very much fun. This is why we want you to be very creative when lettering. Try using your pens to write in a script style. Or, how about trying an outline style using different colors for the insides? (See pages 20 through 23 for examples.)

In this chapter we show you how to make different types of letter styles. You can even combine the letter styles to make fun designs. Once you see how much fun lettering can be with felt tip pens you will want to make your own greeting cards, posters and more. We have given you examples, but you can create any style you want (well, almost anything!).

Remember, use your imagination and **have fun!**

Felt Tip Lettering

Markers are great for lettering. Try the techniques shown here to letter your own name. You might also see fun lettering styles in magazines or other books. Experiment — lettering can be fun!

Here are four basic styles of lettering:

SERIF

A B C D E F G H I J
K L M N O P Q R S
T U V W X Y Z
a b c d e f g h i j k l
m n o p q r s t u v w
x y z

SANS SERIF

A B C D E F G H I J
K L M N O P Q R S
T U V W X Y Z
a b c d e f g h i j k l
m n o p q r s t u v w
x y z

ITALIC

A B C D E F G H I J
K L M N O P Q R S
T U V W X Y Z
a b c d e f g h i j k l
m n o p q r s t u v w
x y z

SCRIPT

A B C D E F G H I J K L
M N O P Q R S T U V W
X Y Z
a b c d e f g h i j k l m n o
p q r s t u v w x y z

Letter Your Name

1 Use light pencil and a ruler to draw horizontal guidelines, as shown.

2 Use light pencil to letter your name between the lines.

3 Trace over the pencil lines you want to keep with felt tip pens. Experiment with wide and thin pens and different colors. You may want to try outlining your name with a thin felt tip pen, then adding a gray shadow with a wide marker.

4 When the ink is dry, erase the pencil guidelines.

SANS SERIF LETTERING

THIN

JASON

WIDE

JASON

OUTLINE

JASON

OUTLINE WITH SHADOW

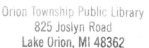

SCRIPT

Jessica

Jessica

SCRIPT WITH SHADOW

Cassidy

Cassidy

**DECORATIVE WIDE SCRIPT
WITH OUTLINE**

Kim

FANCY SCRIPT

Tiffany

Tiffany

Combine Letter Styles

Now we will combine different letter styles to create some fun designs. Use your imagination!

SERIF ITALIC

SANDY

SERIF

BRIAN

SERIF OUTLINE

SCOTT

OUTLINED WITH A SHADOW

Colorful Invitations

Use a variety of letter styles and different colors to make fun party invitations. We used tracing paper and permanent markers to make our example, but you can use any kind of paper and pens you choose.

1 First decide what you want to say. Then use light pencil and a ruler to draw horizontal guidelines on a piece of paper, as shown.

2 Use light pencil to letter your invitation (use the horizontal lines as guides).

3 Lay a piece of tracing paper (or any paper you can see through) on top of the penciled letters. Use felt tip pens to trace over the pencil lines you want to keep. You can use wide or thin pens, in any color. Remember, this is just an example. Use your imagination to create your own design! (You may want to try different styles by tracing over cards you have received in the past.)

4 If you choose, you can decorate your invitation by adding spots of color.

5 Fold a piece of colorful construction paper in half to make a card, then glue the tracing paper to the front.

Who could resist this party invitation!?

Book Cover

Use felt tips to make a colorful book cover.
It's fun and practical!

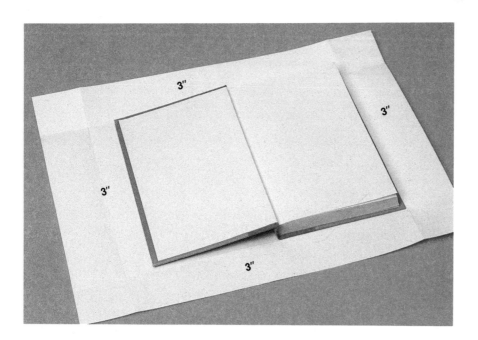

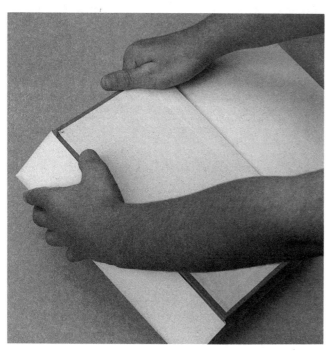

1 Measure the width and length of an open book, as shown. (You may want to ask an adult for help.)

2 Add six inches to each measurement. (Three inches on each side and at the top and bottom.)

3 Cut out a piece of construction paper the width and length you need.

4 Fold the paper three inches down from the top and three inches up from the bottom.

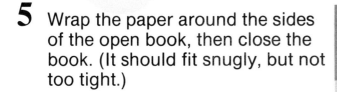

5 Wrap the paper around the sides of the open book, then close the book. (It should fit snugly, but not too tight.)

6 Take the cover off and lay it flat again.

7 Noticing the fold marks, use light pencil and a ruler to draw horizontal guidelines, as shown.

8 Use light pencil to letter the name you want on the outside of the book (use the horizontal lines as guides).

9 Use felt tip pens to trace over the pencil lines you want to keep. Use any colors and types of pens you want.

10 When the ink is dry, carefully erase the pencil guidelines.

11 Now decorate your book cover by adding designs of color. Use your imagination!

Now you're ready to use your one-of-a-kind book cover!

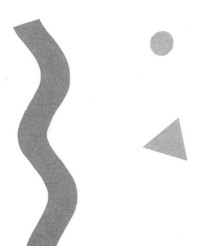

Art Tool Box

We used an empty oatmeal box to make this art tool box. You can also make a fun box for jewelry, toys, special trinkets, photos and cards, or anything you want.

1 Find a box that will hold your art supplies. (Get permission if the box does not belong to you.) Remove the outside wrapper or label.

2 Measure the box with a ruler, then cut a piece of construction paper the width and length you need to cover it. (Check it by wrapping the paper around the box.)

3 Cut out a piece of construction paper one inch wider than the lid. (This will allow one-half inch all the way around for gluing.) Cut slits all the way around the circle, as shown.

4 Cut out a strip that will wrap around the edge of the lid, covering the glue of the lid wrapper.

5 Use light pencil and a ruler to draw horizontal guidelines on the paper, as shown.

6 Use light pencil to letter your name and the words "Art Tools" on the part of the paper that will be on the outside of the box. (Use the horizontal lines as guides.)

7 Use felt tip pens to trace over the pencil lines you want to keep. Use any colors you want.

8 When the ink is dry, carefully erase the pencil guidelines.

9 Now decorate your box cover by adding designs of color. Use your imagination!

10 Glue the box cover to the box.

3

MIXED MEDIA

In this chapter we experiment with mixed media techniques. We make some great gifts by using various media and by being creative. We show you how to make both two- and three-dimensional art projects using felt tip pens and your imagination.

The first project is a two-dimensional drawing of a tiger. You can draw any animal or anything else you can dream up. We also show you how to make a three-dimensional mobile. This time we made parrots. Can you think of other fun mobiles? You can even make an abstract mobile out of fun shapes.

One of our favorite projects is the window hanging. Did you know that you can use felt tip pens on clear plastic and it will look like stained glass? We also show you how to make a puppet and original, colorful wrapping paper.

Remember, whatever you make, use your imagination and **have fun!**

Jungle Tiger

We used water-base and permanent felt tip pens to make this jungle tiger. These techniques can be used for any subject — use your imagination!

1   Use light pencil to draw the tiger on a piece of watercolor paper. (You may want to refer to our *Drawing Fun* book.)

2   Use a wide, water-base marker to color in the basic colors. Leave some areas white. When you have created the look you want, carefully erase any pencil lines that show.

3   Shade the tiger by coloring a brown line in the areas you want shaded.

4 Color the leaves and the ground using different shades of green and brown.

5 Add some orange to the ears and the nose. Color the eyes.

6 Use a medium-soft paint brush to carefully brush water over the water-base marker colors. This will cause the colors to bleed. Now your drawing looks like a watercolor painting.

7 You may choose to frame your drawing by gluing it onto a colorful piece of construction paper.

What a fun way to create watercolors!

Butterfly Window Decoration

We used construction paper and acetate to make this butterfly "sun catcher" window decoration.

1 Choose a design that you would like to make into a window decoration. You can draw your own, copy from another book, or trace our example.

2 Find a piece of acetate or clear plastic. It must be thicker and stronger than kitchen plastic wrap and it must lay flat, like paper. (You can buy clear acetate at most hobby and art stores.)

3 Place the acetate over the drawing you want to trace. You may want to tape it down if you can do so without damaging the book or the drawing you are tracing.

4 Color in the solid areas of the design with permanent markers, as shown. Use any colors you want.

5 Use a black permanent felt tip pen to trace the outline of the design onto the acetate.

6 When you are finished outlining the drawing, cut it out. We chose to cut a circle around our butterfly, but you can cut any shape you want.

7 Cut two identical shapes out of construction paper to frame your drawing. The construction paper shapes should be one-half inch wider than the plastic shape. then cut our identical holes one-half inch smaller in the middle of the construction paper so the plastic drawing can show through. This one inch border of construction paper will overlap and frame the plastic.

8 Glue one piece of the construction paper frame to one side of the plastic drawing. When the glue is dry, glue the other piece of the paper frame to the other side of the plastic so it frames the drawing from both sides.

9 When the glue is dry, punch a hole at the top of the frame and attach a string to it. Hang the decoration near a window so the sun can shine through the plastic.

Gift Wrapping Set

We used water-base markers to make this unique gift wrapping paper.

1 Tape a large piece of newsprint art paper (not newspaper) or tissue paper to a smooth, dry surface. Make sure the tape and the water will not damage the surface. (Get permission if the table does not belong to you.)

2 Tape a small piece of newsprint art paper (the gift tag) to the surface.

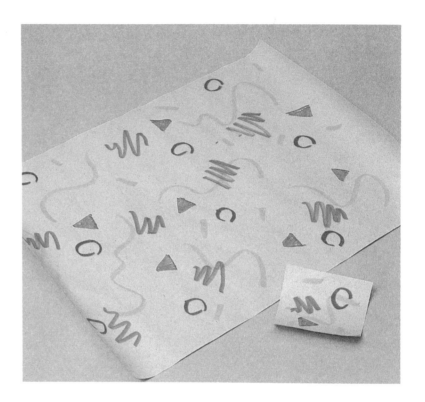

3 Use colorful, water-base felt pens to draw squiggles and designs all over both pieces of paper.

4 Use a soft, wet paint brush to brush and drip water over the papers as shown. The water will cause the colors to bleed.

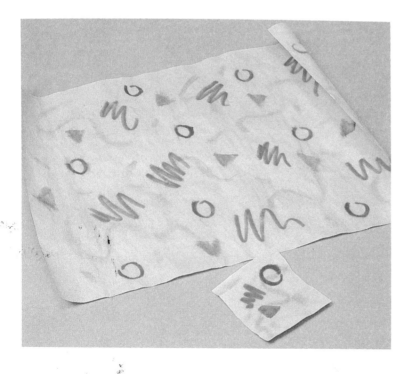

5 Let the paper dry.

6 If you choose, you can trim your gift tag so the colors go all the way to the edge. We also glued ours to a piece of colorful construction paper. Punch a hole in the tag and attach a piece of string to hang it on the present.

7 When the paper is completely dry you can wrap a present.

Which is more fun — the present or the wrapping?

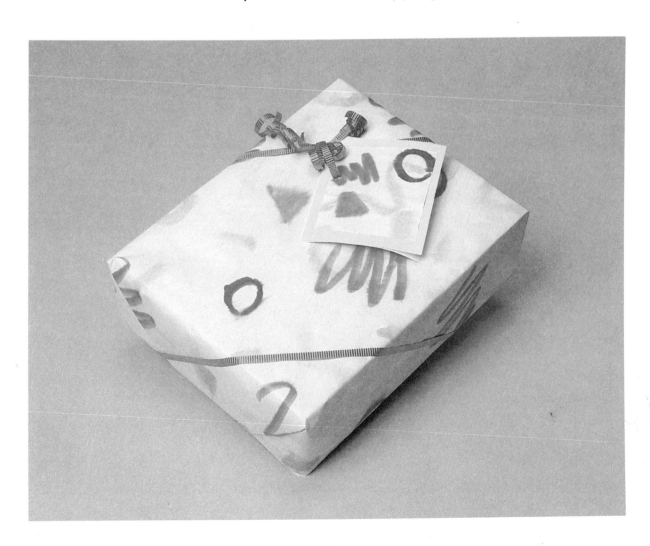

Paper Bag Puppet

We used a brown paper lunch bag and heavy white drawing paper to make this cute puppy dog puppet.

1 Using light pencil, draw two ears, two eyes, a tongue, and a tuft of hair on a piece of heavy white drawing paper. You can copy our example or use your own designs.

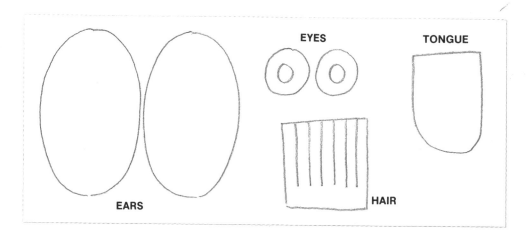

2 Use felt tip pens to trace over the pencil lines you want to keep. Then color in the parts of the puppet. When the ink is dry, erase any pencil lines that show.

3 Use felt tip pens to make spots on the brown bag. We made black spots and put one over one of the puppy's eyes.

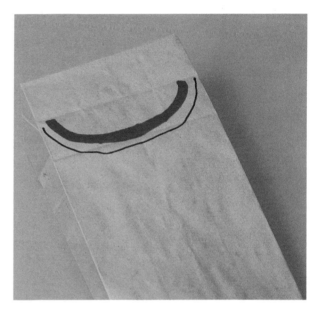

4 Draw a nose and a mouth on the bag.

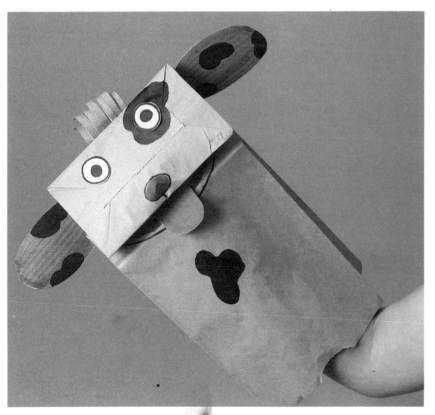

5 Cut out the eyes, the ears, the tongue and the tuft of hair and glue them onto the bag.

Get ready for your puppet to come to life!

Parrot Mobile

We used heavy drawing paper and water-base markers to make this fun parrot mobile. You can make a mobile of any subject or design you want.

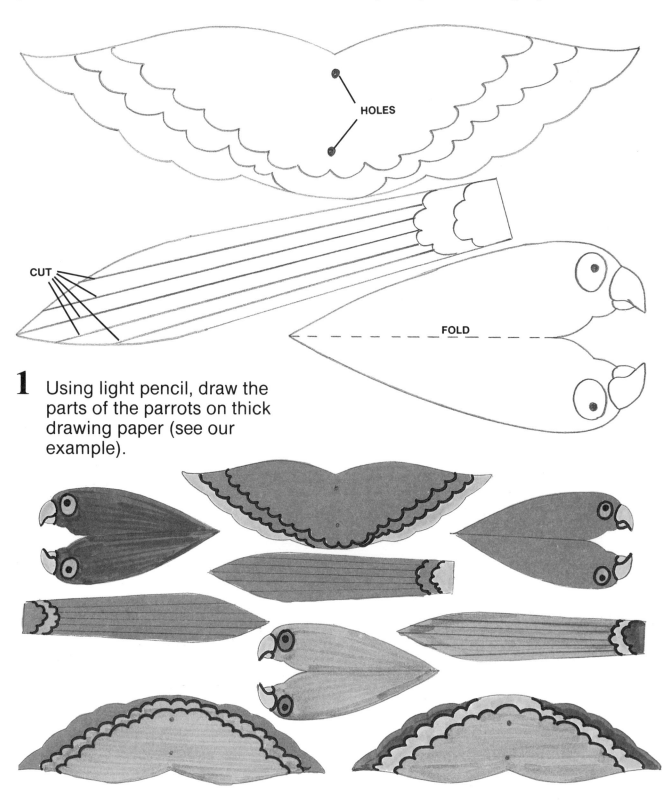

HOLES

CUT

FOLD

1 Using light pencil, draw the parts of the parrots on thick drawing paper (see our example).

2 Trace over the pencil lines with different colors of felt tip pens, as shown.

3 Color in the solid parts of the parrots.

4 Cut out the parrot shapes.

5 Punch two holes in the center of the back of each parrot's wings.

6 Glue the parts together, as shown.

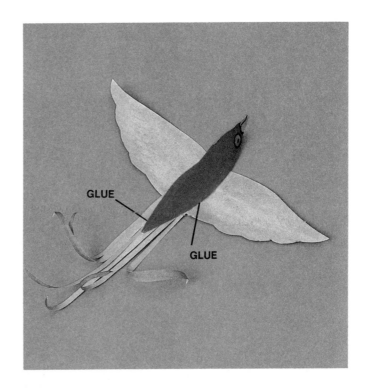

GLUE

GLUE

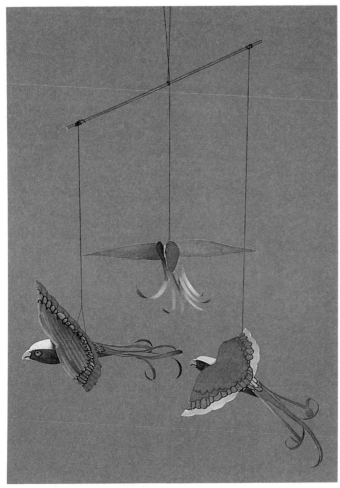

7 Curl the tail feathers by wrapping each one around a pencil.

8 Attach a piece of string to each parrot.

9 Attach the other ends of the strings to a plastic straw or a stick. Make sure the weight is balanced. (This can be done by making all the parrots the same size and all the strings the same length.)

10 Attach another piece of string to the center of the straw and hang it up.

Now you have a whole flock of pet parrots!

4
HOLIDAY FUN

We like to create projects when we're home from school (or work) because of a holiday. We have a lot of fun holiday ideas in this chapter. We use felt pens to decorate plastic cups for holiday punch and to decorate Easter eggs (you can create eggs that are really unique). We also made a monster mask for Halloween, a May Day basket with pretty paper flowers and, for the most fun of all, an advent calendar for Christmas (you can make a calendar for any occasion). Our Christmas calendar gives you a chance to use your imagination by creating different projects to do while you're home from school.

Remember, all holidays provide opportunities for sharing (even on scary Halloween you give candy). And the very best presents or surprises are the ones that have been handmade using your imagination. **Have fun!**

Christmas Cups And Place Mats

This is a fun activity for any party. You can change the design to suit the holiday. You will need some disposable plastic cups for this project. Be sure to ask permission if they don't belong to you.

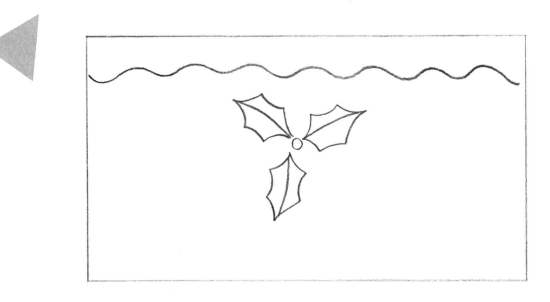

1 Experiment by drawing holiday designs in different colors on a piece of scrap paper. Which designs and colors do you like best? We chose to draw holly leaves in green and red.

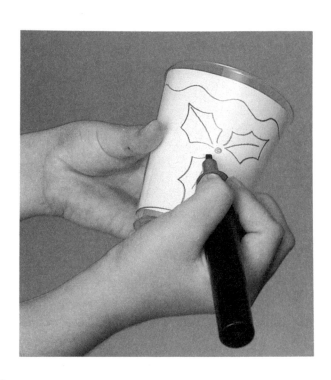

2 To keep your cup clean (the natural oils from your hand can cause the felt tip ink not to stick) you may want to hold the cup at the top and bottom.

3 Using fun holiday colors, draw your design on the side of each cup. If the cups are clear, you may want to put your original drawing inside of each cup and trace the designs on the outside of the cup. (This will help you make all the designs look the same.)

4 Use the same design you used on the cups to decorate the corners of the place mat (you can buy plain paper place mats at a party or stationery store). Remember to draw your design in light pencil first, then trace over it with felt tip pens.

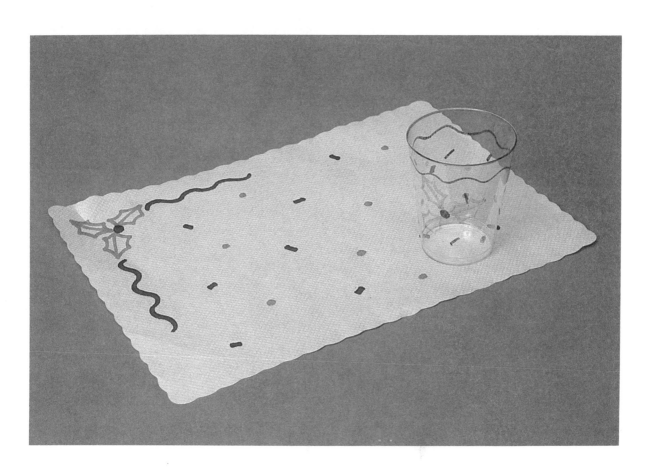

Easter Eggs

You probably already know how to dye Easter eggs, but did you know that you can decorate them with felt pens, too? Try it! It's fun! (Be sure to use non-toxic markers.)

1 Hard boil some eggs and let them cool. Dry them off with a paper towel, if necessary. They must be completely dry or the ink from the felt tip pens won't stick.

2 You might want to practice drawing designs on a piece of drawing paper first. Use bright, Easter colors.

3 To keep your eggs clean (the natural oils from your hand can cause the felt tip ink not to stick) carefully hold the eggs at the top and bottom with your fingertips.

4 Choose fun colors of felt tip pens to carefully draw designs on each egg. Use your imagination!

These eggs look too good to eat!

May Day Basket

We used tissue paper and water-base markers to make this decorative basket. This is a great project to make for any occasion, as either a gift or to put a gift in.

1 Find a basket that has not been painted or varnished. (It should look dull and natural.) Be sure to get permission if the basket does not belong to you.

2 Select your color scheme, then carefully color the basket with permanent markers, as shown. You may want to plan out your design before you begin.

Decorations For The Basket

1 Use masking tape to tape a piece of tissue paper to a flat, dry surface. Make sure the tape and the water will not harm the surface. (Get permission if the table does not belong to you.)

2 Use light pencil to draw the flowers and the leaves on the tissue paper.

3 Use water-base markers to trace over the pencil lines, as shown.

4 Following the shape of the flowers and leaves, use a soft, wet paint brush to brush water over the flowers. This will cause the colors to bleed, making the flowers look soft.

5 Let the paper dry, then cut out the flowers. Twist the center of the flowers, as shown, then carefully open each flower.

6 Glue the flowers onto the basket.

7 Cut out the leaves and glue them onto the basket.

8 Let the glue dry completely.

What a pretty May Day basket!

Advent Christmas Calendar

It's always difficult to make it through the last few days before Christmas. This project should help make the time go by faster! You can have fun making this calendar and then have fun opening it each day before Christmas.

1 Use light pencil to draw a Christmas tree on a heavy piece of drawing paper or bristol board.

2 Use felt tip pens to trace over the pencil lines and to color the tree and the tree decorations.

3 When the ink is dry, carefully erase any pencil lines that show. You may want to frame your tree by gluing it to a colorful piece of construction paper.

4 Draw twelve circles on a separate sheet of paper. Number the circles from one to twelve. Color and decorate them any way you want.

5 Cut out the circles.

6 On the back of each circle write an activity to do each day. Use your imagination. One day you may want to give somebody a candy cane, another day you might want to do a chore for someone in your family. Fido might even enjoy a holiday brushing one day.

1. Make Christmas cards for everyone.
2. Load the dishwasher.
3. Hide candy canes for everyone. (Remember where you hid them!)
4. Make Christmas decorations for the tree.
5. Make hot chocolate for the family.
6. Help fold the laundry.
7. Draw a fun cover for my book report.
8. Rearrange my room.
9. Give Mom a chocolate.
10. Make popcorn for the family.
11. Feed Fido for Sis.
12. Make cookies.

7 Punch a hole in the top of each circle and a hole in the tree where each circle will be attached. Attach the circles to the tree with yarn, ribbon or string, as we have. What a fun way to count down to Christmas!

Monster Mask

A mask is great fun at parties — especially Halloween parties.

1 Using light pencil, draw a monster face on a large piece of construction or newsprint art paper (not the same as newspaper). Make sure the paper is large enough to cover your face and shoulders. Our example is oversized for even more fun.

2 Use felt tip pens to trace over the pencil lines you want to keep, then color in the face.

3 When the ink is dry, carefully erase any pencil lines that show.

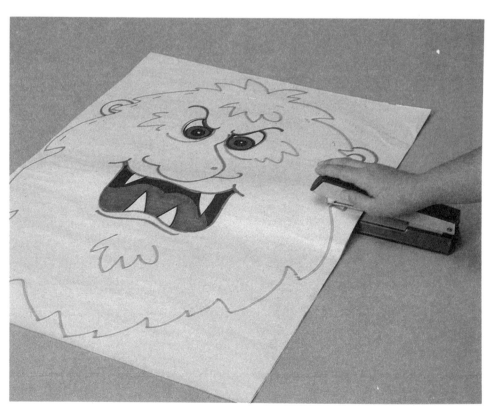

4 Cut out the mask along with an identical piece of plain paper. Staple the edges of the mask to this piece of paper — but don't staple it at the bottom! The paper will support the mask and make the mask into a "bag" that will fit over your head.

5 Try on the mask and decide where your eye holes should be. (You might want to ask somebody to mark them for you.) Cut out the eye holes.

Now you're ready to scare all those other witches and goblins.

ITALY · SWITZERLAND · FRANCE · GERMANY · UNITED KINGDOM · IRELAND

the History of the Leprechaun

Leprechaun (Pot of Gold)
The leprechaun is an Irish mythical character (at least we've never seen one.) The name probably comes from the two word luchorpan, which comes from the Old Irish words lu (small) and corp (body). Usually The leprechaun is told be a mischievous, little man dressed in green, (some say his body is actually green, which perhaps is where the legend of the alien little green men comes from). The Irish believed (and some still do) that if you could catch a leprechaun you could make him tell you where the rainbow ends. As so it follows that if he would tell you where the rainbow ends, you would find a pot of gold there that the leprechaun has hidden. Of course, legend has it that the leprechaun is very quick and tricky. Being green makes it easy for him to hide in the lush landscapes of Ireland.

Because he doesn't want to be caught, he usually out smarts anyone hunting for him. When he has been caught (although the authors have never witnessed this) he can usually challenge his captors to solve a riddle which of course, they never can. So as elusive as the end of the rainbow is, so is the leprechaun. At least we've never heard of anyone finding the pot of gold at the end of the rainbow.

54

5

FUN SCHOOL PROJECTS

You may think that school projects aren't fun, but, have you ever made a volcano diorama with red-hot lava oozing out of it? Or, have you ever researched the history of a holiday to see how it got started? Or, when you're studying a foreign country, have you thought about drawing the country's flag as a school project? Well okay then, you're about to find out that school projects can be fun!

One of the best ways we know to get a good grade while having fun is to do an original school project. The next time you do a report you may want to include a drawing such as a flag or map. Teachers usually like the variety of something artistic and they also appreciate the extra effort.

Remember, as with all learning, you're limited only by your imagination. So be creative, and most of all, even when it's for school, **have fun!**

Flags

You can learn about flags of the world while you have fun drawing them. What a fun school project!

1 Choose flags of the world that you would like to draw or that you are studying in school. A school text or an encyclopedia will have colored examples.

2 Use light pencil and a ruler to draw your flags on watercolor or construction paper. You can draw them all on one piece of paper or on separate pieces.

3 Trace over the pencil lines with colored felt tip pens. Try to match the colors of the real flags as closely as possible.

4 Color in the solid areas of the flags with matching colors.

5 When the ink has dried, carefully erase any pencil lines that show.

6 Cut out each flag.

7 Glue one side of the flag to a stick (flag pole) or a straw as shown.

8 Display the flags by arranging them and gluing them onto a heavy piece of construction paper or an art board.

9 Neatly letter the name of the country underneath.

Looks like an "A" project!

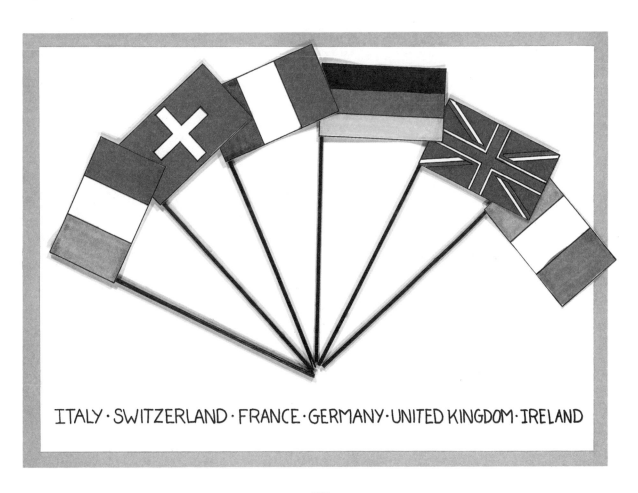

ITALY · SWITZERLAND · FRANCE · GERMANY · UNITED KINGDOM · IRELAND

St. Patrick's Day Poster

We chose to tell the history of the leprechaun for our project, but you can use a part of any holiday or historical event to make this fun school project.

1 Plan the design of your poster before you draw or paste anything onto your paper.

2 Use light pencil to letter the poster. (Refer to chapter 2.)

3 Use light pencil to draw your leprechaun. Be sure to leave plenty of room for the story.

4 Use felt tip pens to trace over the drawing and the lettering.

5 Color in the solid areas of your drawing.

6 When the ink is dry, carefully erase any pencil lines that show.

7 Glue the story on the poster. (To make your story neat, you may want to type it.)

8 You may choose to frame your poster by gluing it to a colorful piece of construction paper.

Leprechaun (Pot of Gold)
The leprechaun is an Irish mythical character (at least we've never seen one.) The name probably comes from the Old Irish word luchorpan, which comes from the two words lu (small) and corp (body). Usually The leprechaun is told be a mischievous, little man dressed in green, (some say his body is actually green, which perhaps is where the legend of the alien little green men comes from). The Irish believed (and some still do) that if you could catch a leprechaun you could make him tell you where the rainbow ends. As so it follows that if he would tell you where the rainbow ends, you would find a pot of gold there that the leprechaun has hidden. Of course, legend has it that the leprechaun is very quick and tricky. Being green makes it easy for him to hide in the lush landscapes of Ireland.
Because he doesn't want to be caught, he usually out smarts anyone hunting for him. When he has been caught (although the authors have never witnessed this) he can usually challenge his captors to solve a riddle which of course, they never can. So as elusive as the end of the rainbow is, so is the leprechaun. At least we've never heard of anyone finding the pot of gold at the end of the rainbow.

59

Volcano Diorama

You can make a diorama of any subject you want. We made ours of a volcano erupting. Copy our example or use your own idea. You will need a shoe box to make this project. (Ask permission if it doesn't belong to you.)

1 Cover the inside and outside of the shoe box with construction paper.

2 Find some books or magazines that have pictures of volcanoes. Decide what kind of background you want to use in your diorama.

3 Use light pencil to draw the volcano, the trees, and the mountains on a piece of drawing paper. Try to make them look realistic.

4 Trace over the pencil lines with felt tip pens.

5 Add details with felt tip pens and color in the solid background areas. When the ink is dry, erase any pencil lines that show.

6 Cut out the parts.

7 Glue the first layer (the sky and mountains) to the back of the box. These are the things that you want to appear farthest away.

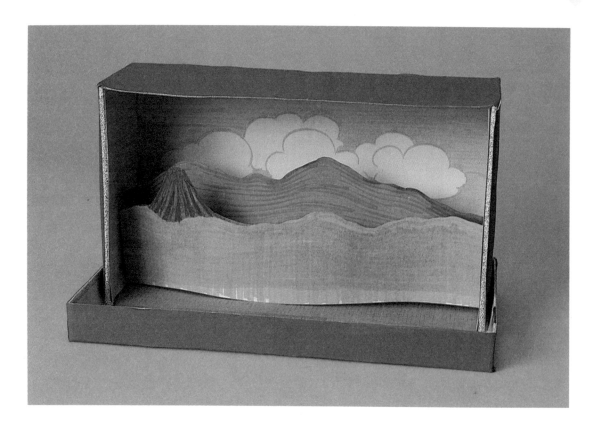

8 Glue the next layer (more mountains and bushes) in front of the first layer by folding the edges of the drawing paper, as shown, and gluing them to the sides of the box.

9 Glue the third layer (close-up bushes, volcano mountain) by folding the edges of the drawing paper and gluing them to the bottom of the box in front of the second layer.

10 We used red felt tip pens on tin foil to make the lava erupting from the volcano. Glue this and any other finishing touches onto the last layer of the diorama.

School projects can be fun!

Beginners Art Series

Walter Foster's **Beginners Art Series** is a great way to introduce children to the wonderful world of art. Designed for ages 6 and up, this popular new series helps children develop strong tactile and visual skills while having lots of fun! Each book explores a different medium and features exciting "hands-on" projects with simple step-by-step instructions.

- **Drawing Fun** begins with basic shapes children know, and progresses to instruction on shading, shadows, and perspective.
- **Color Fun** teaches the fundamentals of color theory: color identification, color mixing, and color schemes.
- **Clay Fun** demonstrates clay sculpting techniques, and acquaints children with several different types of clay.
- **Comic Strip Fun** teaches children how to draw facial expressions, body movements and character interaction.

- **Poster Fun** introduces basic design and lettering skills, then uses these techniques to create posters, greeting cards, and games.
- **Paper Art Fun** shows how to create a variety of paper art objects from everyday materials like construction paper and paper bags.
- **Cartoon Fun** teaches beginning artists how to use simple shapes to create cartoon characters.
- **Painting Fun** teaches the fundamentals of painting with watercolor, acrylic, oil, and poster paints.
- **Felt Tip Fun** demonstrates the use of a variety of felt tip and marker pens through projects ranging from two-dimensional art to a puppet and a diorama.
- **Colored Pencil Fun** offers a series of two- and three-dimensional art projects which help children learn fundamentals such as shading, color blending, and basic drawing.

Age	5	6	7	8	9	10	11	12	13	14
Drawing Fun										
Color Fun										
Clay Fun										
Comic Strip Fun										
Poster Fun										
Paper Art Fun										
Cartoon Fun										
Painting Fun										
Felt Tip Fun										
Colored Pencil Fun